ABOUT T

Nick Jones has been getting big laughs on the circuit for a few years now. But when he isn't out running, he likes to write jokes.

Nick is a proofreader and copywriter. He lives in Cheshire with his wife, son and three cats.

INTRODUCTION

There are a few people I must thank for their invaluable contributions to this book. The first is my editor and close friend, Ben Corrigan. As well as improving many of the jokes with his helpful suggestions, he kindly allowed me to use a couple of his own. The book is much sharper as a result of his input, and Ben is a very funny man in his own right. He's also very charming and intelligent. Thanks, Ben, for editing the book so thoroughly, especially this paragraph.

Thanks to Tiffany Sheely, my talented illustrator whose brilliant cartoons really bring the visual gags to life, and to my good friend Chris Curley for designing a great cover.

I must also give a big thanks to Richard, my brother, for acting as a sounding board for many of the jokes that appear in the book. He also wrote a couple himself.

Thanks to my darling wife Claire who has tolerated me during the four months that it took me to write the book, and to my wonderful son just for being there. Lucas, this book is for you – I really hope you enjoy reading it when you're older.

Thank you also to my friend Ian Maclachlan and my old man, Mike Jones, for giving me permission to use a couple of their gags.

And now for some special mentions. It's important that I give a huge shout-out to my Aunt Ethel, because she's hard of hearing. And I'd also like to express my gratitude to all those who have ever attended one of my self-awareness courses – you know who you are.

Finally, thanks must also go to you, dear reader, for taking the time to read my silly little book. I hope you like it. One tip: in my experience, joke books lose their effectiveness if you whizz through them too quickly. Read it in short bursts and you're laughing – hopefully!

DEDICATION

When I told people I was writing a book of my own jokes, a few of them said, 'Over my dead body.' This book is for you; may you all rest in peace.

NICK JONES

GAGGED AND BOUND

My mum gave birth to me whilst completely submerged in sugar. I was born with Silver Spoon in my mouth.

Last night I jumped off a building, crashed through a roof and landed in an old pub. It was a bit of a dive.

I told my mate I was struggling to meet women. He said, 'Why don't you go dancing? You've got that great move.' But after taking his advice, I've had even less luck. It's one step forward, two steps back.

Apparently everyone at Pixar fell out when *WALL-E* was released. Then they all kissed and made *Up*.

When my girlfriend dumped me we had to divide all our possessions, and I got the GPS system. I was heartbroken but at least I knew where I stood.

My grandmother always used to say, 'The way to a man's heart is through his stomach,' which is why she lost her job as a cardiac surgeon.

Don't you hate it when people leave a football match before the end so they can avoid traffic? Our goalie's always doing it.

There's an Irish goalkeeper that does it too, but that's a Given.

My uncle's in prison for flashing. He says he can't bare it anymore.

Have you heard about the man who spends all his time riding on buses? Seriously, where does that guy get off?

I spent three days in a sauna once. I would have left sooner but I wasn't feeling too hot.

A friend and I once tried watching recorded quiz shows for 24 hours in a row. My friend got bored so I cut to *The Chase*.

I came home the other day to find that a burglar had broken in and stolen my external hard drive. He really got my backup.

If tightrope walking is called funambulism, walking must be ambulism. But where's the fun in that?

It's really important to obey the laws of grammar. Rules is rules.

My friend said to me, 'Have you ever seen a Tennessee Williams play?' I said, 'Yes, I've seen Serena at Wimbledon. It doesn't get more tennisy than that.'

I went through a phase recently where I seemed to keep hitting the ground running. Then I realised I was just running.

This guy once said to me, 'Hey, do you run the Ministry of Arithmetic, Fractions and

Formulas?' I said, 'Yeah, why?' He said, 'You do the MAFF.'

A circle goes into a bar. The barman says, 'What can I get you?' The circle demands a gin and tonic. The barman says, 'I'm happy to get you a drink, but you're going to have to calm down.' The circle says, 'I'll calm down when you get me a gin and tonic.' The barman says, 'Look, I will get you a gin and tonic, but you're going to have to calm down first.' The circle says, 'I WILL CALM DOWN WHEN YOU GET ME A GIN AND TONIC.' It's a vicious circle.

I asked my friend a question while he was eating an orange. I got a pithy response.

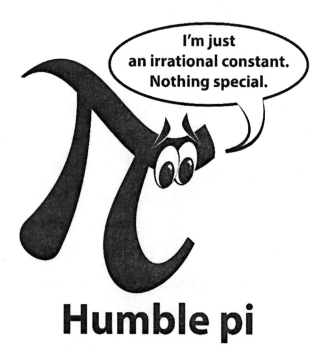

Humble pi

Why did the businessman get sacked whilst on secondment? He was acting office head.

Who was the most agreeable man in history? William the Concurrer.

Who was the second most agreeable man in history? Yessir Arafat.

Bob: Is it true that your local high street is frequented by muggers?
Barry: I wouldn't bank on it.

I've got an idea for a novel about a town in Staffordshire, but it's not set in Stone.

Sign writers. They have their work cut out.

When I visited Ben Nevis, the top was completely obscured by fog. I couldn't see the point of it.

My wife insists that I make her toast to go with her boiled eggs. If I get the timings wrong, she gives me the cold soldier.

I went to a climbing centre the other day only to find that someone had stolen all the grips from the wall. Honestly, you couldn't make it up.

A couple from London have been jailed for a month for gently rubbing themselves against passengers on the tube. Some say they got off lightly.

Did you hear about the owl who lost his voice? He couldn't give a hoot.

My great grandad was the first person to use foil to keep his house warm. He said it came to him in a flash of insulation.

I rang my friend the other day and when he answered he said, 'Hi, I'm stood next to a bed of nails at the moment.' I said, 'Don't lie.'

There's talk of a wet T-shirt competition taking place in our local village. I'll be the judge of that.

Did you hear about the guy who was born with no buttocks? He wasn't really arsed.

I've got a load of batteries you can have if you want? No charge.

Would you be interested in a load of tyres as well? No pressure.

Do you want to buy my brewery off me? 100 grand, no vat.

I've got a special offer on hens. Battery's not included.

I've got a great deal on windows and doors too. No catches.

I've got a load of yo-yos if you want them? No strings attached.

Heat a frying pan over a medium heat, add pine nuts and toast them for a few minutes until browned and fragrant. Place chunks of parmesan in a food processor and add basil leaves, garlic, the toasted pine nuts and olive oil. Season to taste with salt and freshly ground black pepper. Blend for a few seconds until it begins to come together and is smooth, and hey, pesto!

Police censuses. They tick a lot of motorists off.

A business owner recently claimed that he has never had a client ring him to complain. When asked what his secret was, he said, 'The customers always write.'

Bob: Have you had many girlfriends?

Barry: I've been out with the odd one.
Bob: Yeah, we've all been out with her.

I tied my son's shoelaces up for him once and he's never undone them since. I went to the school of hard knots.

Let's take turns to name every American Vice-President. Al Gore first.

A man goes into a pub. He walks up to the barman, who is standing behind a wall that is one foot tall. He says, 'This joke has set the bar too low.'

I've looked up to my dad ever since he took a job as a trapeze artist.

By day I'm a bus conductor, by night I play the villain in a pantomime. My life's tickety-boo.

I tried drag racing the other day. It's murder trying to run in heels.

Did you hear about the kid who fell into a lion's enclosure with his Compare The Market toy? It cost him an arm and Oleg.

Wolverine. He's a man of many talons.

The council are threatening to build houses on my dad's allotment. I'm worried he might lose the plot.

What's the correct way for a servant to answer

a duck?

'Yes, Mallard?'

Did you know that Cat Stevens has five drinks of tea a day, all of varying sizes? The first cup is the deepest.

The world stilt-racing champion needs a new supply of stilts. He's running low at the moment.

A woman came up to me and asked me if I'd help her with her vajazzle. I said, 'I'm not going to dress it up for you – the answer's no.'

I tried hunting geese last month. Once they started flying, I knew the game was up.

My friend eats so much stone fruit that he can no longer pronounce the letter 's'. He says he has a peach impediment.

I went to pick up my car from the garage. As I approached it I noticed the tyres were flat. I checked the oil and it was empty. Then I checked the windscreen wash and brake fluid – both empty! I went up to the mechanic and said, 'Oi, mate, I think you've done me a disservice here.'

I went to the doctor for a test result. He said, 'I'm going to give it to you straight.' I said, 'OK, but I'd like the test result first.'

A coat of arms

I've just been to the butcher's and bought a topside of beef. I might have been able to manage a bigger cut, but I didn't wanna brisket.

I went to a meeting for sufferers of Chronic Fatigue Syndrome, and someone cracked a joke about the condition. When I took offence, he assured me he was laughing with ME, not at ME.

My computer's so old that when I upload data to it, I have to do it in byte-size chunks.

In the new series of *Postman Pat*, he has a mobile phone, a laptop and a helicopter. It's postmodern.

Do you know what's really eye-catching? Conjunctivitis.

I saw Alistair McGowan make his debut on the stage. First impressions weren't very good.

Why are protons and electrons always content? Because they're in their element.

I'm training for a marathon by jogging 10 miles a day. It's really tiring but it'll be worth it in the long run.

Bidets. They're too lavish for me.

Football pitches. People swear by them.

Me and my mates were in a frenzy last night. It's like a onesie but all your friends can get in it.

I've just landed a full-time job making vases. For the first time I'll be on Pay As You Urn.

Do you struggle to keep your eyes open after using your iPad? There's a nap for that.

I tried to have a conversation with my wife when she was applying a mud pack. You should have seen the filthy look she gave me.

I went to the pub last night and afterwards I queued for a taxi. There were puddles of vomit on the ground, but there were also tubs of flowers in full bloom. So, overall, pretty rank.

A batsman collapsed and died during a cricket match, just one run away from victory. His friend said, 'It was a terrible loss, but at least he had a good innings.'

My friend has chiselled features. That's what you get when you pick a fight with a sculptor.

After a long week of work, me and my mates like to get together and develop computer-generated images. We call it CGI Fridays.

Then on Saturday nights, the wife and I go down to the canal, and I use my finger to propel baby hens into the water. My wife loves watching chick flicks.

Why hasn't Sean Connery ever been to France?

Because every time he asks to go to Paris, he ends up in his local church.

When I was in India, I saw a man sitting cross-legged playing a tune to a snake. I thought to myself, 'That's charming, that is.'

A gay friend of mine took me to the Mardi Gras festival last year, followed by a Marc Almond gig and a night in Soho. After all that I couldn't think straight.

I've got a wonky voice. I can only sing in one key.

I was on a plane with my girlfriend when she said, 'Listen, I need to tell you something. Before I met you, I was dating a pilot, and once

I slept with him in the cockpit whilst he was flying a plane.' I shrugged and said to her, 'Well, at least you've been upfront.'

Did you hear about the boy who was made of sausages? Pork kid.

My friend's head has a cannon on the front that turns 360 degrees. He's got turret syndrome.

Diabete, diabete.

Type 2 diabetes.

I just watched half an hour of *Hamlet* on TV with the sound off. That was a hard act to follow.

A guy just came up to me screaming and shouting whilst holding out a giant bird. I said, 'Alright, mate! Keep your heron!'

The other day I was driving to a country pub to meet a friend for lunch. I hadn't been there before and I got a bit lost, so I pulled over and asked a man for directions. He looked at me suspiciously and said, 'Oh yeah? Why do you want to go there then?' I thought this was a very odd reaction, but I went ahead and explained that I was meeting a friend there. He looked at me for a long time and then sighed and said, 'Go to the end of the road and turn right, then go straight on for a mile.' I thanked him and drove off, following his directions, but when I got there, there was no pub, just an old lady stood on the pavement. I pulled over and asked her for directions to the pub. She scowled at me and said, 'Hmmm … What's your reason for going there?' Again I explained that I was meeting a friend. She looked me up and down and eventually said, 'OK, go left, then right, go over the roundabout and then go on for fifty yards.' I did this, and again there was no pub there, but there was a man stood on the side of the road. Totally bewildered by this point, I stopped and asked the man for directions. Again I got the same reaction, but finally this time the man's directions got me to the pub. When I went in, my friend said, 'You took your time! What happened?' So I told him about all the odd people that I'd seen on the way there, and he smiled and said, 'Ah. You went the cynic route.'

Did you hear about the guy who was eaten by a shark? When he was buried, it was just two feet in the ground.

My son is really naughty, so I've bought him a book called 'Train yourself to be polite.' That'll teach him.

I was a bookkeeper for 10 years. The local library weren't too happy about it.

The other day I walked past a plain white billboard with a policeman standing in front of it. 'Nothing to see here,' he said.

There's something about my left hand. It's not right.

I've put everything I own on a horse. There's a lot riding on it.

My dog was always chasing his tail so I make him wear a cone collar. He hasn't looked back since.

I poured a can of lemon-and-lime soft drink over my head the other day. I felt spritely after that.

Why did the lady ask Dennis Quaid to move his car? Because he was *Innerspace*.

Bob: Can I have some of your sleeping pills, please?
Barry: Knock yourself out.

How long does a squirrel look for food? Forages.

My friend was tapping away on a calculator, so I asked him what he was working out. He said, 'I'm obtaining values by dividing the sum of several quantities by their number.' I said, 'Meaning?' He said, 'Yes.'

I went to the park the other day, but when I got there I realised I'd forgotten to bring the dog. I wasn't with it.

I'm thinking of buying 500 jiffy bags on eBay.

I've got a lot on my mind.

My grandad just found out he needs to have a pacemaker fitted. He's broken-hearted.

How do trainees carry out tasks? Interns.

Apparently Pedigree Chum have brought out pecan-flavoured dog food. It's the mutt's nuts.

I was at a rock gig with my mate and he turned to me and said he wanted to go crowdsurfing. I told him not to get carried away.

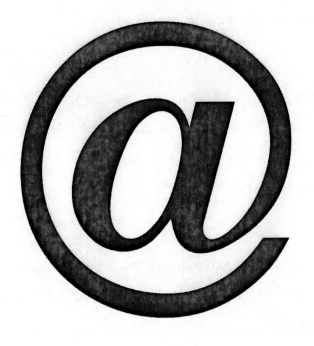

This page is full of character.

A couple of Barcelona's players have been struck by a nasty stomach virus. The club doctor says it could get Messi.

My friend had to have a leg amputated, and now he suffers from phantom limb. He says he gets this weird feeling but he can't put his finger on it.

Why were Charlie, Juliet and Mike behaving so crazily? They were part of the frenetic alphabet.

I've got a photographic memory. Well, I've got a camera with an SD card.

A man goes in a bar. The barman says, 'Does anyone know who this mango belongs to?'

Patient: Doctor, is there anything you can do for my asthma?

Doctor: Don't hold your breath.

A friend was telling me about this serial killer ventriloquist who has a puppet called Ducky. His defence in court was that Ducky talks to him and tells him to kill people. After telling me all about it, my friend said, 'So what do you think?' I said, 'I hope they bang him up and throw away Ducky.'

My dog swallowed my mobile phone so I had to ring his neck.

I went to work the other day and everyone in the office was telling each other off. Then I remembered it was dress-down day.

I get my hair cut at Moses Barbers. They do one style: waves with a parting.

I once refereed a game of darts between the world's tallest blind men. It was all above board.

When you think you've found your perfect match but the spark has gone, it's time to stop dating matches and try humans.

A man was sent to the psychiatric hospital with the delusional belief that he was made of rubber. Over the course of the next week his condition deteriorated – suicidal, he climbed on to the roof and was threatening to throw himself off. The doctors said not to worry; they were sure he'd bounce back.

I was discharged from hospital the other day. I was only visiting a relative, but all the exit doors were jammed so I had to leave via the laundry chute.

Some people just can't take losing an argument. The other day I was trying to have an intelligent conversation with someone, and he totally spat his dummy out. Then he threw his toys out of the pram. Then his mum slapped me round the face and told me to pick on someone my own size.

I'm studying with the Open University. So far we've learnt about yards, miles and hectares. It's a distance learning course.

Some people totally defy convention. For

example, my wife's a petrolhead, whereas other women's heads are made of flesh and bone.

There's been an outbreak of a stomach bug which causes violent vomiting. I went to the doctor's and the place was heaving.

Be careful what you wish for

Boy: Dad, I think it's disgusting that you and Mum have sex.

Dad: You don't have to tell me – I'm the one who has to do it.

I ordered a Subbuteo team from Tesco online and it was delivered with no substitutes.

I got forty winks this afternoon. I was sat on the bus opposite a girl with a nervous tic.

I'm always accidentally adding an apostrophe when I abbreviate the Department of Health. D'OH!

When I was a child, I had the idea of trying to teach my hamster to walk down the stairs. It was short-lived.

I spent ages trying to revive it, but in the end I had to knock it on the head.

A genie once popped out of a lamp and slapped me in the face. I said, 'What did you do that for?' He said, 'You rubbed me up the wrong way.'

Has any man ever proven the existence of Bigfoot? Not yeti hasn't.

Two ants are having an argument on a wall calendar. One says to the other, 'Carry on like this and I'm gonna knock you into the middle of next week!'

Have you ever been fly tipping? It's like cow tipping but far less strenuous.

My friend, who's hard of hearing, said to me, 'Don't you think it's disgusting when people use derogatory terms to describe disabled people?'

I nodded and said, 'Defo.'

I told a tree a scary story once. It was rooted to the spot.

A lazy i.

What do you call a booking agent with cancellations? Disconcerted.

Bob: If I told you to jump off a pier, would you do it?
Barry: Probably, yeah.
Bob: That's pier pressure for you.

Someone stole my chessboard and all but one of the pieces. Now I just sit around and watch pawn all day.

I attended a course of Weight Watchers sessions, but it wasn't exactly a success, for any of us. At the end of the final session, it was happy faces all round.

Son: Dad, you know how your arm goes to

sleep if you lie on it long enough?

Dad: Yeah.

Son: Well, the same thing just happened with the hamster.

Bob: These hallucinogens are so strong I can't feel my legs!

Barry: You don't have legs, you're a goldfish.

This French guy just came up to me and uttered 'nine' in his native language. Neuf said.

Someone stuck a wiretap on the outside of my jacket. Daft bugger.

How does Derren Brown make a car move backwards without touching it? Reverse psychology.

I flew one of those seaplanes the other day. It was difficult landing it on the water, but it was plane sailing after that.

A bar went into a man. It was a Mars bar.

They say 'Charity begins at home'. But our daughter is called Charity and she was born in a hospital.

A Dutchman has invented shoes that record how many miles you've walked. Clever clogs.

Bob: Have you seen that film *Total Recall*?
Barry: I can't remember.

Why is a joke like sex? It's not funny if you don't get it.

I did a presentation to a class of children using a projector. It went right over their heads.

A man goes into a bar and says to the barmaid, 'I want to pick your brains.' The barmaid says, 'Sorry, all we sell is Guinness, Becks and Stella.'

Wife: Where are you going?
Husband: Um, there's no easy way to say this.
Wife (worried): What do you mean?
Husband: Well, I'm going to Llanfairpwllgwyngyllgogerychwyrndrobwlllla ntysiliogogogoch to meet Frank.

My dad always gives sound advice. He's a sound engineer.

He has to do a lot of 1-2-1s at work. And he's always getting 360-degree feedback.

Bob: What's this white thing? It's boiling!
Barry: It's a boiler.

A local business has been dubbed 'the laziest company in the UK' by its customers. The CEO reclined to comment.

Magic eye pictures. I don't get what people see in them.

I've been trying to write a joke for each letter of

the alphabet. I thought I was funny, but it will be more amusing when the joke's on U.

Nasty stomach bug? I'm down with that.

Don't tell a comedian to eat his words – he might end up with gag reflux.

By the time my niece was 12, she'd written over a hundred books. The local library weren't too happy about it.

Due to the recession, thousands of forklift truck drivers are struggling to find work. They'll need things to pick up soon.

What do cats say when they self-harm? Me-ow.

I offered a cannibal a sweet once. He nearly bit my hand off.

I hate rubberneckers as much as anyone, but they've got one thing going for them: no risk of whiplash.

My ex-girlfriend must be psychic. When I rang her to tell her I didn't want to go out with her anymore, she said, 'You're breaking up,' and put the phone down on me.

I had an argument with my friend when we were on a fairground ride. After some toing and froing, we realised we were going round in circles.

Another time we were having a debate whilst sat in a sauna. Things got a bit heated.

And then there was the time when we were arguing over who caused a forest fire. He started it.

The day my wife walked out on me, I didn't know what had hit me. It was only later in the hospital that I found out it was a frying pan.

Do you know what I find unnerving? Root canal surgery.

A man walks into a bar with his dog. The landlord shouts, 'Hey, we don't allow dogs in here.' The man says, 'Come on, he's not bothering anyone.' The argument heats up until the landlord shouts, 'Do you wanna take this outside?' The man replies, 'No I don't, that's the whole point, you idiot!'

What's ambience? It's what someone with a tongue injury asks for when they ring emergency services.

Did you hear about the pessimist who tried to establish a career as a lumberjack? He felled miserably.

Why is Dracula more creative at night? Because he gets to think outside the box.

I once played a cricket match in which parts of a Mr Potato Head were used instead of cricket balls. No one batted an eyelid.

What did Tony Christie say when he went to the zoo? 'Is this the way to the armadillo?'

I split up with a girlfriend after going rock climbing with her. Too clingy.

Bob: I heard about your date with my sister. Is it true you stood her up?
Barry: I had to. She was so drunk she couldn't do it herself.

I've had a fan installed in my cranium. Mind officially blown.

How do church ministers make jam from fruit? They pulp it.

I just beat my friend in a pancake-making competition. He reckons he should have won because he added lemon juice, but I think that's just sour crêpes.

Bob: I went to a district of Liverpool last week.
Barry: Speke?
Bob: I just did.

I let my friend borrow my grandfather clock. He owes me big time.

What was Pac-Man doing in the empty maze? Looking for a spot to eat.

Servant: Your highness, the traitors have been put to death and are now on display on London Bridge.

Henry VIII: Thanks for the heads up.

I used to walk past a busker every day, and he always played *Greensleeves* on his flute. One day I asked him, 'Why do you always play the same song?' He said, 'I only like that one song and I have no intention of ever learning any others, OK?' A few weeks later, as I approached the busker, I was surprised to hear that he was playing *Hey Jude*. 'You changed your tune,' I said.

My wife's a professional wine taster. She's wasted in that job.

She tried to find an accountant but apparently there's no accounting for taste.

Bob: Have you seen the news? A policeman is on the beam of a big steel bridge, trying to coax a woman down!

Barry: Cantilever?

Bob: No, he's worried she might jump.

I like to have a large mug of Earl Grey just before I go to bed each night. It's not everyone's cup of tea. Just mine.

The mug I use is lined with gold paint. It's my gilt tea pleasure.

I was in the park playing with my son, and this little girl came up to us. She grabbed my son by the cheek and started dragging him away. Before I could react, the girl's mother shouted: 'Emily! Stop that! How many times do I have to tell you that it's rude to pull faces!'

Have you ever used one of those Pez sweet dispensers? Flippin' neck!

Andrew Lloyd Webber tried writing *Andrew Lloyd Webber the Musical*, but he couldn't compose himself.

I'm playing in the Tetris World Championships next week. I'll be bricking it on the day.

Harvey Kite-Tail

My friend just won an award for best cameraman and another for best original music. He shoots, he scores!

Bob: I went to a town in North London for a haircut.

Barry: High Barnet?

Bob: No, short back and sides.

Why was the horror novel lying in a hammock? It was chilling.

Things always get lost in translation between my wife and me. The other day she tried on a dress and asked for my opinion. I said I thought it was abysmal, and she went and bought the next size up.

You know what really sticks in the memory? A USB flash drive.

What's the first sign of madness? 'You are now entering Birmingham.'

Patient: Doctor, I haven't been feeling myself recently.
Doctor: Brilliant! The therapy must be working.

Due to a production error, a signmaker has printed some of the Fiat logo with some of the Tesco logo. The company has apologised for the fiasco.

A guy in the pub told me that he sells clockwork toys for a living. I don't know whether to believe him, though; everyone I've spoken to says he's a wind-up merchant.

Bob: I've written a 400-page short story.
Barry: That's novel.

Mum: Billy has been suspended from school again for taking a pornographic magazine into class.
Dad: Oh, not again! Honestly, I don't know where that boy gets it from.
Mum: I do. I just found the box in your wardrobe.

I've just been to the National Pessimists' Society conference – try that for sighs.

Ivana Trump is thinking of getting her initials

tattooed on her scalp. On her head be IT.

Why do funeral directors only drive their hearses in the slow lane on the motorway? So they can keep undertaking.

I saw two mice in suits turning other mice away from a mouse hole. I realised later that they must have been dormice.

Every year for my wife's birthday, I take her to visit an ancient Roman stronghold. It's the fort that counts.

What do you get if you cross expensive perfume with cheap television? Channel no. 5.

I've got a pet donkey that listens to Dr Dre, smokes marijuana and stays out all night. He's such a badass.

Customer: Do you sell Wotsits?
Shop assistant: Can you be more specific?

Patient: Doctor, I have a headache and my vision has gone blurry.
Doctor: You should have gone to Specsavers.

Why didn't the mice mistrust their big-nosed, big-handed brother? They thought he might be a mole.

What happens when herbs get into debt? They receive a visit from the bay leaf.

Two ducks are swimming in a river. One says to the other, 'That new film's out today. I'm gonna fly to the cinema. You coming?' The second duck replies, 'You go ahead. I think I'm gonna stream it.'

If you take your watch to a jeweller to be fixed, don't pay them upfront. Wait until the time is right.

Why did the young farmer spend a lot of his time at agricultural shows? Because it's a great place to pick up chicks.

Once upon a time there was this man who cocked the hammer on his gun and pulled the trigger. It's a cock and pull story.

How does a caravan feel when it goes on holiday? Ex-static.

I met my wife doing a street survey. She ticked all my boxes.

Bob: Is there a way of holding back the entire Atlantic Ocean?
Barry: Dam strait!

I went to the market the other day to buy some fruit. When I got to the fruit and veg stall, I noticed that all the bananas had the ends chopped off. I asked the stall owner why, and he said, 'We've got a special offer on at the moment – a third off all bananas.'

Why do the military use an X to pinpoint a

tyrant's whereabouts on a map? Because X marks despot.

What do you call a snake wearing a hard hat? A boa constructor.

Interviewer: When you're playing in a tournament, what drives you on? Golfer: My buggy.

What did the policeman shout at the thief who'd raided a butcher's? 'Put your hams where I can see them!'

Doctor: Your tests have come back, and it would appear that you have an Atrial Septal Defect.
Patient: I believe you hole-heartedly.

Every time my friend goes to board a plane for his holidays, he gets in a scuffle with the staff and gets banned from the airport. It's his fight-or-flight response.

Racecourse assistant: Do you think the greyhounds would race faster if we introduced a mechanical rabbit to the course? Racecourse owner: Good idea! Let's run it past them.

I just watched the National Asthmatics Society's charity run. They made it look so wheezy.

I was going to set up a multinational clothing retailer, but there's already a Gap in the market.

What type of rock is never delivered on time?
Slate.

Fisherman 1: What's your best pick-up line?
Fisherman 2: Probably the one I'm holding.

People used to always say, 'Pigs might fly,'
and then what happened? Swine flu.

Boy: Dad, I've just had confirmation that I've
been accepted for the Mars mission!
Dad: That's great, son. I always wanted you to
go far.

When I'm playing board games I have a never-
say-die attitude. I just think dice sounds better.

Why was the fishmonger both pleased and exhausted after his stock check? Because he found mussels he never knew he had.

I always like to put my own stamp on things. The local library aren't too happy about it.

I got bored of my collection of keyboards so I painted them all pink. They haven't been the same synths.

Which fruit gets claustrophobic? Betternot squash.

Apparently, if you've been involved in an accident that wasn't your fault, you might be entitled to compensation. I'm thinking of suing my parents for my conception.

When times are so hard that you find yourself in a supermarket, staring longingly at the OXO but with no money to buy any, it's time to take stock.

I'd never sign up to a human-cloning programme. I don't think I could live with myself.

My father uses ambiguity to hide his gambling addiction. I'm no better.

How does the tide rise? Slowly but shorely.

What usually happens the morning after a one-night stand? Goes without saying.

NICK JONES

Two brothers are playing golf. The younger brother hasn't played before and keeps losing his golf balls. After a while, his brother gets fed up and says, 'You should practise with old balls in future.' The younger brother replies, 'I'll tell Dad you called him that.'

The company I work for have just moved to an open-plan office. I'm not happy about it so I've started a partition.

North Courier

South Courier

I don't trust conversion websites. Give them an inch, they'll take 1.609344 kilometres.

I'm a stay-at-home dad. Whenever my family go out anywhere, they always say, 'Stay at home, Dad.'

Did you hear about the comedian who got 12 strikes in one game of bowling? No pin untended.

I was walking in the countryside one hot summer's day when I saw the wagging tail of an animal sticking out of a bush. I was intrigued so I approached it, but when I got close it withdrew into the bush. I slowly crept into the bush and there it was again, sticking out of another bush. Again it disappeared so I followed it. Soon I spotted it sticking out of another bush, wagging, tantalising me. This went on for about an hour and in the end I was so fed up I just went home. The moral of the story: don't tail tails.

I tried flying a kite the other day and it was impossible. How are you supposed to mount such a small bird?

Why is *Made in Chelsea* like a scrapyard? There are some right toffs in it.

What's precise and sounds like a carrot? Accurate.

My uncle was a butcher, a pastry chef and a cannibal. He had fingers in a lot of pies.

The wife and I are both having laser eye surgery next week. Not sure we're going to enjoy it, but we'll see.

Why did the tramp deliberately sleep on wet paint? He wanted to set a new benchmark.

Bob: My grandmother was a touch typist. Barry: That's nice. My grandad was a touch racist.

Have you seen that new fantasy film about a big flying white creature with chronic gum pain? It's called *The Nerve Ending Story*.

I got arrested by a blonde policewoman last week. It was a fair cop.

I bought a budget grammar guide. You pays your money and you takes your choice.

Do you remember when dyslexic jokes were all the rage? That was a bad spell.

I messed around so much at school that I had to retake my History GCSE three times. It's true what they say: 'Those who do not learn from history are doomed to repeat it.'

My doctor upset me last week. He told me I required a suppository and I took it the wrong way.

My uncle used to say, 'Sticks and stones may break my bones but names will never hurt me.' Until he walked past IKEA and the logo fell off and crushed him to death.

Did you know that terns are monogamous birds? Hence the phrase, 'One good tern deserves another.'

Why does cooking make your arms ache? Because utensil your muscles.

My friend kept whinging to me about her acting career, saying that she's getting typecast as a weak, oppressed woman. I told her she needs to stop playing the victim all the time.

When I'm in the kitchen with my wife and I ask her for the sieve, she always throws it at me. She's pass-sieve aggressive.

If it's true that a good man is hard to find, Wally should have a knighthood by now.

Bob: Do you think your wife would go up in a hot air balloon?
Barry: Of course she would. She's not that heavy.

I bought some energy-saving light bulbs. I was disappointed to find that they took just as much effort to put in as the old ones.

In the Battle of Falmouth in 1779, soldiers protected themselves by sticking a drawing pin in their foreheads. Apparently a tack is the best Falmouth defence.

My son came up to me and kicked me in the

stomach. I fell to the floor and shouted, 'What did you do that for?' He laughed and said, 'You wimp! I kicked mum in the stomach for nine months and she never complained.'

Boy: Dad, Charlie has climbed inside a flowerpot and has covered himself in soil. Dad: Don't worry, son, he'll soon grow out of it.

Which celebrity wrote the ultimate toilet book? Lou Reed.

I went to the dentist for a filling and he told me to sit back and brace myself. I told him I wanted to see a dentist who knows what the hell he's doing.

Reading between the lines

I've got a friend called Allen Key. He's not the sharpest tool in the box.

The other night it was so muggy that I couldn't sleep. It was too close for comfort.

I was too lazy for the army. I went abroad to fight for my country, but came home a week later because I was missing inaction.

I did a comedy routine in a hospital ward. They were all in stitches.

I think steps should be taken to ensure that couples remain faithful. A loyalty card on their wedding day, for example.

I used to be a life coach, which sometimes affects my relationship with my son. One time I saw him playing football with his friends and they were using jumpers for nets, so I told them they needed clear, defined goals.

I've decided to go to Switzerland and put an end to my pain and suffering. I'm sick of always having an inferior wristwatch.

Did you know that Timothy Dalton deliberately played James Bond badly? He thought the director said, 'Always leave the audience wanting Moore.'

The other day I painted one half of my face like a clown and went for a drive in the car. I don't think anyone saw the funny side.

Did you know that if the driver takes child-friendly mode off, lorries swear when they reverse?

Whoever coined the phrase 'What goes up must come down' clearly never tried collapsing a pop-up tent.

I need to have a leg amputated and I'm thinking of going private. It's a one-off payment.

I think my wife is stupid. She told me I was one sandwich short of a picnic, and I wasn't even going on a picnic!

Why do microwave cooking instructions tell you to stand for one minute at the end?

Trench warfare. It's a bit over the top for me.

I was such an unlikeable child that even my imaginary friend talked about me behind my back.

I used to be best mates with a gingerbread man – that was short and sweet.

I like slides but I don't like see-saws. It's all swings and roundabouts.

At one time in my life there was a price on my head. I was playing 'Who Am I?' and the answer was Katie Price.

Modern life is so easy. Years ago, if you

suspected someone of being a witch, you threw them in water to see if they float. Now all you need to do is buy *Witch?* magazine.

I have a drum kit which I play with my hands. Can't beat it.

How do you catch an online predator? Lol them into a false sense of security.

I've invented toilet roll which has a story written on each sheet. Read it and wipe.

Dyslexic jokes are sikc [sic].

TV shows like *Police, Camera, Action!* must be a great deterrent to criminals. They show that even if you have a really blurry face, you won't get away with it.

I think I'm in love with my gloves. Whenever I wear them I get that warm, fuzzy feeling.

When I was little I asked my dad for some money and he gave me a cheeky backhander. I couldn't sit down for hours after that.

When I saw a man trying to break into my car, alarm bells started to ring.

Taxidermists. They know their stuff.

Ashley Cole is the two-time world champion.

Massage parlours. That's a touchy subject.

Doctor: How many fingers am I holding up?
Patient: Feels like three to me.

Bungee jumping would be torture for a lemming.

I've just heard that vandals have stolen the F from the Funfair sign in our town. Now that is just unfair.

'I've cracked it!' shouted the inventor of the nutcracker.

'How many times do I have to tell you?' thought the speaking clock.

'Where have you been all my life?' said the adopted child to his birth parents.

When my grandad died, my mum told me to put on a brave face, so I wore a gladiator mask to his funeral.

Doctor: We successfully removed the tumour from your brain.
Patient: Phew, that's a weight off my mind!

I bought the complete set of Encyclopaedia Britannica the other day. That says it all.

My wife's bell-ringing group were so bad that when they disbanded they won the Nobel Peace Prize.

I got arrested in a library last week. The policeman said, 'You have the right to remain silent.'

Did you hear about the tall leprechaun? All he wanted was to be short to be short.

Why do customers say to waiters, 'I like my steak well done!' before they've even ordered it?

Why are abacuses upright? So they can stand up and be counted.

Bob: What do you do for a living?
Barry: I run a business with my son. I do front of house, he does back of house.
Bob: Oh, you run a restaurant?

Barry: No, we're window cleaners.

How do you trick a horse? Feed it Shergar cubes.

My friend has made a counterfeit stamp. I advised against it, but he forged a head anyway.

I once lit a magnesium strip in a chemistry lesson without the teacher's permission. You should have seen the reaction I got!

Builder: We've installed the new revolving door for you.
Site owner: Thanks for the quick turnaround.

Never hit a man wearing glasses. He might break them when he hits you back.

Patient: Doctor, whenever I get money out at a cashpoint, I feel sick and my head hurts.
Doctor: Sounds like you're having withdrawal symptoms.

I'm a big supporter of suspended animation. *Thunderbirds* was particularly good.

Nose studs. They're a bit in your face.

On a hot summer's day, I like to drink G&T without the gin. It's just the tonic.

Patient: Doctor, I feel like a Russian

playwright.

Doctor: Chekhov?

Patient: No, but I sneeze occasionally.

Smoking e-cigarettes is the safest way to take ecstasy, apparently.

After 24 hours of creating the universe, God decided to call it a day.

When my son turned two, his most-used phrases were 'more' and 'again', which is funny because at that time my most-used phrases were 'no more' and 'never again'.

Why do some fish swim on their own? Because they're too cool for school.

My son tears his hair out at bath time, so we tried that No More Tears shampoo. It didn't work.

I didn't like playing tag at school. Too slapdash.

I've got googly eyes. They're always searching for something.

Whenever Robinson Crusoe had that Friday feeling, he'd punch him and run away.

Patient: Doctor, every night I sleepwalk into the bathroom, get the talcum powder out and rub it all over my body.
Doctor: Don't worry, it's common to talc in your sleep.

Batman Biggins

Sometimes being anally retentive is a good thing. When smuggling drugs, for instance.

How do two cartoonists decide who's best? They draw lots.

Bob: I was in a room earlier and it was 180 degrees on the inside.
Barry: Blimey. Fahrenheit or Celsius?
Bob: Neither, I just meant there were only three walls.

I bought a new strimmer today. It uses cutting-hedge technology.

My friend says I'm obsessed with similes. What's he like?!

iPads. They get a lot of press.

Bob: I'm reading *The Bridge over the River Kwai* – the unabridged version at the moment. Barry: Is it called *The River Kwai*?

ITV are doing a new show about the life of Arthur Daley when he was a kid. It's called *Child Minder*.

Did you hear about the guy who pretended he was going to steal a jumper from a clothes shop? He was just trying it on.

How many proofreaders does it take to change a ~~lightbulb~~ light bulb?

I perform a mime version of Matt Damon and Robin Williams' Oscar-winning film. I call it *Good Will Gesture*.

When it comes to learning, our son is in a class of his own. It's for the good of the other pupils, apparently.

If Death set up a sewing business, there could be some serious reaper cushions.

What's a hobo when it's at home?

The big bang. That's a blast from the past.

When a dog runs round in circles, why do we assume it's chasing its tail? Maybe it's running away from its teeth.

Bob: Which part of a swimming pool do you like most?
Barry: Deepends ...

Brain surgery. It's not rocket science.

Whenever I ride my bike, a priest appears beside me shouting, 'The power of Christ compels you!' It's an exorcise bike.

Is there another word for thesaurus?

I used an alarm clock for the first time this morning. It was a real eye-opener.

My friend asked me to give him some feedback on his CV. He handed it to me and I noticed it had a huge E printed over the front of it. I said to him, 'Why have you written a huge E over the front?' He said, 'That's my covering letter.'

Bob: Would you sign up for cryonic preservation?
Barry: Yeah, why not – you only live once!

When we met, my wife was a Bunny Boiler. It's better now we're married – people don't laugh at Bunny Jones so much.

Westlife must have one-track minds because all their songs sound the bloody same.

My aunt is a schizophrenic and she's really

dull. She's always boring people.

I tried having a conversation with someone via an intercom. It was like talking to a brick wall.

A footballer died recently, and at the funeral his team-mates arranged for a red card to be placed in his coffin. They wanted to give him the ultimate send-off.

What wears a crown, barks and claps? The Royal Seal of Approval.

My son likes to make cowboys out of his Lego. He's a cowboy builder.

My mate's known to the police as a repeat

offender. It's not his fault he's got Tourette's syndrome and a stammer.

How does James Bond feel after a night on the vodka martinis? Shaky, not sturdy.

What should a mother do if she finds her child unbearable? Have a C-section.

There used to be a market for an ultra-thin plastic bag, but then the bottom fell out of it.

I'm always holding back in my job. I'm a chiropractor.

Return tickets. They take me back.

Which of the Mr Men is unluckiest in love? Mr Bounce, because he's always on the rebound.

What's the best treatment for lockjaw? Keyhole surgery.

My cat has a chip on his shoulder. It should be between his shoulder blades but the vet slipped.

Bob: You should get a GB sign added to your car registration.
Barry: I've got enough on my plate, thanks.

I had a bit of rumpy pumpy last night. I was choking on my steak and someone had to perform the Heimlich manoeuvre on me.

Did you hear about the time Dr Dolittle tried to break up a fight between two dolphins? He soon realised that he was talking at cross porpoises.

I went on a date with this woman who wasn't all there. She'd left her glass eye at home.

A well wisher

My mate designed the doors for Warwick Davis' house. He was told he had to keep them low-key.

He's also got a sideline business with me, manufacturing door hinges. It's a joint venture.

I think Simon Cowell's parents must have said, 'Belt up!' a lot to him when he was a child.

I'm a big fan of crazy golf, or as I like to call it, silly putty.

Since *Father Ted*, Channel 4's attempts at sitcoms have all seemed feckless to me.

Fortune cookies. They're not all they're cracked

up to be.

My wife just won a year's supply of Warburtons products, which makes her the main breadwinner in our household.

I once got locked in a cupboard with a giant chess piece. It was a long knight.

I just watched a film about a tug-of-war team. The story was a bit ropey.

Have you ever seen a snake eat a large animal whole? Jaw-dropping stuff.

I can't decide whether we are all driven by a will to power or whether we're shaped by events around us. It's the old Nietszche vs. nurture debate.

Have you ever seen the pilot episode of *Mr Benn*?

My mate gave me a dead arm, which is why he lost his job as a mortician.

In school, I had a debate with my chemistry teacher and he blinded me with science. He was so annoyed he threw acid in my eyes.

I'm really getting into horse riding. I've been three weeks on the trot.

What's green, covered in children and presents

The Cube? Philip Schoolfield.

Every dog has its day. It's called International Dog Day.

Why do criminals with stammers never leave prison? Because they can't finish their sentences.

This joke's about incense. It's a slow burner.

Did you hear about the man who tried to give himself a sex change? He couldn't pull it off.

Team GB were recently surveyed regarding proposed cuts to their funding. The synchronised swimmers voted with their feet.

Why did the penguin storm out of the pub in a mood? He couldn't hold his drink.

Apparently someone's just been arrested for making jokes about other people's misfortunes. I shouldn't laugh …

Did you hear about the teenagers who broke into an *X-Factor* judge's mansion? They partied till the Cowells came home.

Bob: I just saw a crab on the sidewalk. Barry: Crabs always walk like that.

I tried to set a new world record for the most people carried on one person's shoulders. It was going really well at first, but then it all fell down around my ears.

I was an assassin for a while. I made a killing.

Which comedian can get you a great bargain on a quality car? A Lexus Sale.

My daughter is an expert on cotton fabric trousers. I taught her everything chinos.

What did the dentist say to the little battery? 'Say AAA.'

I had a huge build-up of wax in both my ears. It was a near-deaf experience.

I took my ill cat to the vet. He spent a few minutes examining it and then, with a glum face, went to pour a jar of syrup on it. I stopped him and said, 'It's OK, I know the cat's dying. There's no need to sugarcoat it.'

When Frank Wynn and Suzanna Wynn got married, neither of them needed to change their name. It was a Wynn-Wynn situation.

I've written a self-help book for people trying to lose weight but it hasn't been very successful. It's called *Help Yourself.*

I was in a pet shop looking at some hamsters. Each one was in its own cage, climbing up the bars as if vying for my attention – except for one that was just sat in the corner of its cage quietly. It all made sense when I noticed a label on the cage that said 'Reserved'.

I just bought the latest issue of *Car Parts Monthly*. It's a bumper edition.

I was walking up the stairs to my flat when I passed a physics student playing with a slinky. I said, 'Hi, how's it going?' and he said, 'A mix of gravity and kinetic energy.'

Did you know that Tina Turner has a sister called Paige? She's a best-selling novelist.

A company has just brought out a tennis ball machine designed for midgets. They're expecting low returns.

Why is it a drag being a chess piece? Because of all the background checks.

I've just published a cookbook aimed at anorexic people. Next year I'm going to write one for the wider public.

Bob: If we wait in this spot for a minute, a male rabbit's going to turn up.
Barry: What makes you think that?
Bob: Because the buck stops here.

Are you scared that an evil spirit lives in your house? You're not alone.

I have to drive over The Second Severn Crossing every day for work. It takes its toll.

Did you hear about the woman who claimed she had not defecated for a whole year? Turns out she was full of it.

I spent last night holding a clock up to a mirror. I needed time to reflect.

Which party game requires just a tin of ravioli? Pasta parcel.

I bought a new mobile phone today and it came with a car charger, which is a stroke of luck because my car has a flat battery.

Why is T the busiest letter in the alphabet? Because it's always in the middle of something.

Did you hear about the pair of wigs that had lots in common? They were like toupees in a pod.

Apparently 92% of men like to masturbate. Each to his own.

I used to go to school with the guy who invented Velcro. He was a bit of a tearaway.

My mate came round my house, and as we were chatting he started freaking out, saying he was having an out-of-body experience. I told him he could see himself out.

Did you hear about the rapper who had a bad stammer? He went into a toy shop and inadvertently bought 23 yo-yos.

My friend was feeling depressed last Bonfire Night so I took him to a firework display. His face lit up.

I'll never forget the unspeakable acts my uncle subjected me to as a kid. Luckily he's a much better mime artist these days.

As a team-building exercise, a company sent its staff up in a hot air balloon. Everyone was enjoying the ride at first, but then the balloon started losing altitude. Realising that the balloon was about to crash, the MD looked round at his employees one by one, until his eyes landed on a couple of temps. He looked at the temps solemnly and said, 'I'm really sorry, but we're going to have to let you go.'

Did you hear about the parachutist who landed on a football pitch during a match? The referee sent him off for descent.

What did B.A. Baracus say when he ordered a hot curry? 'Pitta the phall.'

My father has gone to pot recently. He's in the final of a snooker tournament.

How did the teacher stop his pupils scraping their fingers down his blackboard? He covered it in No More Nails.

A man ran up to me with a drinking straw in his mouth and pinned me to the ground. I took several blows to the head.

I got trapped in a revolving door once. After a few minutes I didn't know whether I was coming or going.

Doctor (to a trainee): That is, hand on heart, the worst attempt at surgery I've ever seen.

Did you hear about the contortionist who got her nose stuck in her backside? Apparently she was a bit up herself.

I once found a hyena that was stuck in an empty beer keg. That was a barrel of laughs.

Two snowflakes were falling from the sky. As they were falling, they were arguing over the best place to land. In the end they settled on the ground.

What did the American say to Alex Ferguson when he got his CBE? 'Man, you knighted!'

Bob: How much does your barber charge?

Barry: Around £8, off the top of my head.

I just visited my aunt in hospital, and all she did was whinge about the other patients in the ward. The nurse said she'll remain in a critical condition for some time.

A prisoner enters his cell for the first time. His cell mate stares him in the face and says, 'What are you looking at?' The prisoner replies, 'About five years if I stay out of trouble.'

Did you hear about the man who bred caterpillars? All his chrysalises came at once.

Cat owner: As you can see, my cat has a massive growth that is completely covering its anus.

Vet: Don't worry – I'll get to the bottom of it.

I used to keep a wild animal as a pet, until the day I threw a house party and drunkenly left its cage door open. I really let my hare down that night.

What do people write on to tell their loved ones about their holiday? Answer's on a postcard.

I just bought a joke book on Amazon. The book itself was free but the shipping was £3.99. It's all in the delivery.

Train of thought

THE END

APPENDIX

I had an illustration of a human appendix here, but then I discovered that Stewart Francis did that gag in his book. So I've had mine taken out.

THANKS!

Thanks again for buying this book. If you enjoyed reading it please tell the world by writing a review on Amazon!

For the latest news on the author please visit gaggedandbound.net or follow @nickjonezy on Twitter.

CPSIA information can be obtained at www.ICGtesting.com
Printed in the USA
LVOW07s2005090315

429805LV00035B/2893/P